Vibrate Higher

By Mystic Mae

About the Author

Mystic Mae is a senior coach at Mindset Mastership, a life coaching business based in London, England.

Mindset Mastership teaches clients how human behavior really works.

Through our teaching, we have helped clients worldwide gain a better advantage, to develop themselves and achieve more from life.

We are in the changing lives business.

Want Free Goodies?

Email us at:

mindsetmastership@gmail.com

Find us on Instagram!

@MindsetMastership

MASTERSHIP BOOKS

UK | USA | Canada | Ireland | Australia
India | New Zealand | South Africa | China

Mastership Books is part of the United Arts Publishing House group of companies based in London, England, UK.

First published by Mastership Books (London, UK), 2021

I S B N: 9 7 8 1 9 1 5 0 0 2 0 1 3

Image credits reserved.
Colour separation by Spitting Image Design Studio
Printed and bound in Great Britain

National Publications Association of Britain
London, England, United Kingdom.
Paper design UAP

ISBN: 978-1-915002-01-3 (paperback)

A723.5

Title: Vibrate Higher

Design, Bound & Printed:

London, England,
Great Britain.

“Wherever you go, go with all your heart.”

– Confucius

Table of Contents

Introduction: **What is Vibrate Higher?** 1

Chapter 1: **The Vibrational Energy of the World** 3

Chapter 2: **Universal Vibration** 7

Chapter 3: **Law of Vibration** 11

Chapter 4: **Raising Your Consciousness** 15

Chapter 5: **How Consciousness and Vibration Works** 28

Chapter 6: **Evidence of Vibrational Energy** 35

Chapter 7: **Signs of High Vibration** 44

Chapter 8: **How to maintain a high Vibration?** 50

Chapter 9: **Raising your vibrational energy** 58

Chapter 10: **Habits That Are Lowering Your Vibration** 93

Chapter 11: **How To Swiftly Shift Your Vibration** 105

Chapter 12: **Raise Your Vibration For a More Fulfilling Life** .. 121

Chapter 13: **Spiritual Awareness** 130

Conclusion 136

Introduction: What is Vibrate Higher?

Vibrate Higher is a spiritual awareness book for those who are ready to explore their inner selves and understand the law of attraction. This inspirational read will help you remove negative energy to unlock your deepest, most beautiful self. Vibrate Higher can be used as a guide for finding peace within yourself by understanding that we are all one and the same with our own individual journeys on this planet.

What is my Vibrational Energy?

Your vibration is the energy with which you operate your thoughts and emotions. It's how you feel day-to-day, in the moment good or bad. This Vibrational energy can lead you to take actions that are in alignment with your thoughts and feelings.

Vibrating negatively can lead to destructive behaviour like addiction, emotional outbursts or low self-esteem. Vibrating positively on the other hand leads to constructive actions that help you manifest what it is that you want such as increased creativity and intuition.

Your vibration is unique to you and it can be defined as your signature. A signature is a personal mark or symbol that identifies something as being from you. This can be your name, initials, or logo.

In the same way, your Vibrational Energy is what makes you uniquely YOU and defines how people see and experience YOU.

This Vibrational energy is intricately tiered to you, meaning you are the only one who can control and alter it.

The good news is, by controlling your vibration you have more choice over what you experience in life. Even better news: You CAN change your Vibrational Energy to align with how YOU desire to feel!

What does this all mean?

Put simply, we are ALL vibrating.

Chapter 1:
The Vibrational Energy of the World

The above section described the human experience of vibrational energy and what it is. Now we will explore how the vibrational energy fields of the world surround us.

It is important to note that, just like with the human experience of Vibrational Energy, if these fields exist all around us, it means we are constantly bathed in them. It's how they affect you (and others) which matters most here!

These vibrational energy fields have been scientifically proven by quantum physics experiments and so we must look at this book with as much significance.

Environmental Vibration

The Vibrational Energy of the World that we are surrounded by is not limited to what you feel or see, but also includes frequencies and sound waves coming from every direction.

Imagine how you feel when you hear the sounds of nature. For example, when you hear joyous singing of birds outside your windowsill, to the dreary noise of an airplane flying overhead, or even the fright of loud thunderstorms! As you see all these scenarios have different vibrations. They all make us feel and act in a certain way, and much like how the world around us can do that, so can the vibrations of a person.

The Vibrational Energy or "Vibes" that people emit are like magnets and attract to them what is similar in vibration, whether it be emotional pain, thoughts of inadequacy, or lack thereof. Our emotions dictate our outer world's experience! Therefore, it is so important to start understanding how we can vibrate on a better level.

Personal Vibration

Have you heard someone say, "I feel Lighter" when they have accomplished a certain task, or heard good news? In the similar way, we can feel lighter when we are releasing vibrational energy that is not serving us. This process of Vibrate Higher starts in our own personal vibration and emanates outwards into the world around us.

When you are aligned to your purpose you feel light, fun, warm, and even calm or contentment with it. This is being inline with your soul purpose.

However, when a person is in a negative Vibrational State they will feel disconnected from their purpose, feeling heavy or weighed down, and if this continues for a long period of time they may even start to experience physical pain.

The way we vibrate is multifaceted! Our emotional state alone determines how the law of attraction responds in our lives. This means if you stay on path with your higher vibration, the law of attraction will always give back to you what is aligned with your highest good.

Sometimes, we need to release things that are not serving us. The process of Vibrate Higher starts in our own personal vibration and emanates outwards into the world around us. Therefore, when we are vibrating at a lower frequency it can be difficult to attract our desired outcome.

In summary, when we operate at a higher frequency we are more in tune with our spiritual self and this manifests into attaining what we desire via the law of attraction.

Chapter 2: Universal Vibration

You Vibration is a your state. It is the frequency you are in. As we noted earlier, the universe is in constant vibration, and each item at different frequencies. Responding to your vibration, not only outside of you but also inside. It is within this vibrational state that you make choices and create the life for yourself.

A metaphysical perspective would say that the human is made up of vibrations- the combined vibrational energy that is produced by physical, mental and spiritual aspects. Each of these elements has a specific vibration.

The Vibration of your thoughts and feelings is what you're sending out to the universe. It's not just in these two areas but also from all parts of your body- or more accurately, that are made up based on vibrations within the cells themselves which then radiate outward as a waveform, affecting everything around them.

What is Vibration?

Scientifically speaking in physics vibration is the periodic motion of a body or part of it. The electromagnetic spectrum (EMS) includes all the possible frequencies. It's made up of waves with nodes and antinodes. The EMS has different parts from gamma rays to x-rays including microwaves, infrared light, visible light etc. These to parts are the building blocks of all matter.

Every living organism is vibrating at a specific frequency. In fact, not only are you vibrating but also your thoughts and feelings carry an electromagnetic signature that contains this same information- the vibrations of that particular mental or spiritual state.

Lets break this down; all matter is made of atoms, which are governed by the laws of physics. The electrons orbiting around an atom vibrate at different rates and as a result transfer these vibrations to everything in our universe including us.

And so inside atoms also exist subatomic particles, which are in a constant state of motion. Vibrations that occur at the perimeters of an atom can be converted to frequencies, and these vibrations make up what is called "electromagnetic radiation".

So when a person meditates and in doing so is able to tap into their spiritual self, they're actually making themselves vibrate at a different frequency that transmits these vibrations out into everything around them including other people. And as we know that atoms make up every physical object there's also an effect to us as well as others, as we're all are made up of the same material, atoms.

Therefore, if one piece of matter can vibrate at different frequencies, which mean the other pieces of matter, are also capable.

So we're all able to change our vibrations or frequency by changing and altering what is going on in our minds, which has been observed as a waveform when using an EEG machine. And this law of attraction can be applied to any person if they want it enough.

Vibration is literally the motion of atoms/ molecules that make up every living thing. These atomic motions produce waves. You can't have vibration without movement- and that is something we do in our every day lives.

Here's another example, image how your Wi-Fi signal is stronger when it's within range of the Wi-Fi signal but as soon as you step away, it dies completely. The same goes for our brain waves and frequency- we can't have vibration without movement or that, which creates a waveform. So if there are no "waves" being created then we're not vibrating at all!

Chapter 3: Law of Vibration

What is the law of Vibration?

The law of Vibration is the high level spiritual principle that states everything in the Universe is made up of vibrations and nothing else. Take a rock for example; it's not really "solid" but rather just an accumulation of billions (and trillions) of atomic particles vibrating at different frequencies to form what we perceive as solid matter.

And so in the same way, the Universe is made up of vibrations and nothing else. The elements all connect with each other at the atomic level, and again these are just vibrations.

The law of vibration is a law, which cannot be undone. Meaning that an atom must vibrate in order to be, and anything that is not vibrating must cease to exist.

A way of understanding this law is through the concept of resonance. When a single vibration meets another vibration with the same frequency in space, they create an amplification effect where one increases the amplitude (height) or intensity of another.

The law of vibration is not only the basis for how we create our physical universe, but it also governs what happens to us in life if you are able to understand and use this law properly.

Therefore, creation is the vibration of thought.

The law of attraction is a universal power or force that draws like to like, meaning it will always bring more positive things to you and your life if you are vibrating at a high frequency.

However, this does not mean that by simply thinking positively all the time we can achieve anything in our lives because what you must understand is that your thoughts, words and deeds are all vibrations.

This law works in the physical world just as it does on the spiritual level because everything runs together here on earth.

As you achieve mastery over this law of attraction, which means that you learn to control your vibration and keep it at a high frequency then there will be nothing to worry about because everything will be flowing to you, and anything that is not in alignment with this frequency will find it's way out of your life.

We are all spiritual beings having a human experience here on earth so therefore we must treat one another as such.

Unconscious Mind & Law of Vibration

The unconscious mind is the part that is always working in the background of our conscious mind. The unconscious mind has no judgement, it just knows what we want and then tries to figure out how to get it for us.

It does this by using Law of Vibration which can be a good or bad thing depending on your vibration frequency. It has been said the unconscious mind guides our thoughts, feelings and actions.

However, it's the conscious mind that has control over what we say, do or think which is why in order to raise your vibration frequency you must be aware of the choices you are making and how they effect your unconscious thoughts and feelings as well as those around you.

This balancing of conscious and unconscious thoughts can be achieved through meditation, self-honesty and practicing gratitude.

I have found that once I started to heal the wounds of my past, change my limiting thoughts into empowering ones which are filled with love rather than fear and opened myself up to receiving limitless possibilities from the universe then positive things in life began flowing more freely both for me and what I desired.

Many people confuse the unconscious and conscious mind. The Unconscious mind is where mostly all of our fears, limiting thoughts and beliefs are stored. The Conscious mind can be thought of as the 'boss' that directs us what to do with these unconscious memories and experiences. If we let fear dictate how things turn out then it will always try to keep you safe by not letting anything happen. This means that nothing new can enter your life because it doesn't want to risk anything. The Conscious mind is the key that unlocks this door and allows us to let go of these beliefs so we may evolve in our conscious understanding, be free from fear and experience the joys of living a happier, more fulfilling life.

Chapter 4:
Raising Your Consciousness

How to Raise your Consciousness?

Be aware. There is nothing more powerful than being present in the moment, live authentically and feel everything that you are feeling. This means not letting your thoughts and feelings get suppressed or hidden from yourself, as this will keep them alive so they may continually manifest for years to come.

When we are aware of the thoughts and emotions that come up within us, they're not so scary. We can see them for what they really are - just thoughts or feelings. And you know how to let go of any thought? Simply stop thinking about it! When you're feeling fear arise inside yourself, simply ask yourself to stop it if this fear cannot provide any learning.

What does it mean to Raise your Consciousness?

Raising your consciousness means waking up to the spiritual awareness of yourself and what you are capable of. It's about connecting with all that is in every moment, realizing whom we really are as human beings and sharing this message with ourselves to gain a deep understanding of our own experience.

Essentially, it means to become aware of the law of attraction. (this is huge)

However, most people have two primary belief systems. One is that individuals respond from years of conditioned habits which dictate outcomes, and secondly, we are just creatures who experience life as it comes.

Such beliefs shape the way we live our lives.

The self-fulfilling prophecy is a belief that the results of something will be what you expect from them, whether they are good or bad. If we think positive thoughts and have faith in ourselves then all things seem possible. Understanding how to change our perspective on any situation can alter all beliefs and it's outcomes. Therefore, habitual beliefs often tend to be incorrect and manifest the unwanted outputs and simply reacting to random actions provides no real purpose for our true desires.

And so to bring into line our consciousness with what we desire can then manifest a self-fulfilling prophecy. We can change our lives by understanding how to live from this perspective and then create what we desire, whether it is for ourselves or others.

Raising Consciousness

Your consciousness is made up of the following elements;

- Thoughts, feelings and emotions.

- Beliefs or opinions about yourself and the world around you.

- What we see as important in our lives: what is a priority to us?

Raising your consciousness can be achieved by removing negative energy which manifests itself through thoughts, feelings and beliefs that are not aligned with who want to be, or see yourself as.

A scientific approach to raising your consciousness is to be mindful of what you are thinking and feeling. You may not realise how many thoughts come into your head in a day, but being present with them enables you to catch the negative ones that drag you down - those which contain fear or anger for example - before they take over and have an impact on your day-to-day life.

Catching these daily thoughts and feelings means you can then replace them with more positive ones.

The law of attraction is the idea that by focusing on what we want and feeling great about it, this will trigger a chain reaction in our lives causing us to manifest those things into reality.

Studies have shown how to raise your consciousness with daily practices can have a direct influence on our physical and emotional wellbeing.

Furthermore, by focusing your energy when you're feeling great about something (whether it be through meditation or prayer), this will help to create more of what you want in life. Beliefs are like magnets that attract the things we tell ourselves every day.

Ways to Raise Your Consciousness

Here are twenty-five ways to raise your consciousness:

1. Meditate

You can start by doing just 5 minutes to begin with or more each day and then you should feel less stressed and more in a state of flow.

2. Make time for stillness

This is when you take the time to just being with yourself; think about what's going on currently in your life and how things might unfold. It can also offer clarity or help make decisions for you if it's required.

3. Contemplate how everything you need is already provided to you

Take a walk with no destination in mind, and allow yourself to be guided by the path. When you're lead somewhere that feels good go ahead and stay there as long as possible

4. Speak your truth

Share something about yourself or your life with someone you don't know well. Not only does it help them, but also helps us to be able to open up and share our lives more generously.

5. Take conscious control of your decisions

When you take the time to ask yourself if you're doing what feels right and good for YOU. It's becomes empowering to put yourself first.

6. If you're feeling stuck with a decision, take a break

7. Listen to your intuition and don't second-guess it

Know that if something doesn't work out for you in one place or time that this just means there's more opportunities where those came from!

8. Open mindedness

Being open minded about what you might be missing out on is a crucial step in learning and growing as an individual. Without it, we're not able to learn new things or realize the possibilities of life that are available for us just because we said "no".

When someone from outside of your norm invites you into their world, try your best to understand that they're not really asking for anything from you. They just want to connect with someone and share their story in a way that they might not be able to do otherwise.

9. Remain open minded enough, but don't let yourself become desensitized or numb because of it.

10. Pursue Intelligence

Pursue intelligence, not ignorance. Pursuing what you don't know will only make you a better individual and give you the chance to grow more than if you just kept your life small and unambitious.

Ignorance might be bliss in some cases but it's also one of the leading causes for people feeling stuck or stagnant.

Examples of intelligence:

- Reading

- Listening to lectures and podcasts

- Studying a new language or culture.

Don't let your intelligence die off by choosing not to pursue it when given the opportunity because you might just find yourself living in regret for years on end. A life without curiosity is a doomed one, so always make sure that.

11. Forgiveness

One of the most important and versatile qualities that not only make you a happier person but also helps other people.

Forgiveness is a form of healing for us as well as others around us because it releases negativity from our lives, clears away resentments, and allows both individuals to grow into better versions of themselves.

Forgiving our past from a place of peace and love sets us free to move forward into a new future.

Forgiveness is the key for spiritual growth

It's time to let go, forgive yourself for everything you've done wrong or left undone in your past and release it all from your life so that you can live freely without any regrets.

12. Control Your State of mind

Having the control to switch your state of mind at will is one of the most important skills you can have in your life. This can be done by using the power of your mind and taking control back from any negative thoughts.

One way to accomplish this is through meditation where we can set our own intentions, find peace within ourselves and transform into a better version of who we are on the inside. This is not just about getting rid of negativity but also about being able to be in the present moment without any distractions.

And so through meditation being present enough to be aware of your state of mind can help to have the power to change it.

13. Change Your Belief Systems

We must not only change our beliefs but also often challenge the very systems, which govern our beliefs.

This can be done by first acknowledging that we are not perfect, but rather a work in progress. And then understanding where our self worth and confidence come from. It is also important to understand how certain people or events have affected us so that they do not continue to affect us negatively. Once we acknowledge these

We want to keep hold of the beliefs that bring us joy and happiness, while working to change the limiting beliefs that cause us pain. This can often be challenging because it requires courage and strength.

We must be willing to face our fears, as we fight for what is right in this world.

It can also help if we work on beliefs that are more positive than negative because they will have a stronger effect of raising our vibration by attracting the things we desire or events into our lives, which will positively impact us.

14. Like minded People

It is important to surround ourselves with like-minded people who can support and enrich our lives.

15. Encourages Positive Behaviour

It is also important for us to be in an environment that encourages positive behavior, so we don't replicate the thoughts or actions of those around us. If we are not careful what we allow into our minds will eventually become part of us.

16. Spirituality

Although pursuing a sense of spirituality is a personal choice it can lead us to an understanding of life and our own selves.

Having a deep understanding of our spiritual selves is key to unlocking the law of attraction. It's about finding a deeper understanding for why you are here, who we really are and what your life's purpose is.

17. Explore the Self

This can be done through exploring who you are as well as what your soul wants for its journey

18. Express Gratitude

It is important to recognize the abundance and love in our lives. Expressing gratitude puts us into a state of peace, contentedness as well as alignment with who we are and our journey on this planet.

When you feel gratitude it frees up your energy for more creative thoughts that will help you attract what you want.

19. Act on Desires

Every person has a certain level of desire for happiness. It is important to spend time on your desires, feelings and thoughts in order to find what you want and need.

20. Discovering Your Purpose

There are many ways people use their life's purpose as part of the spiritual journey which leads them closer to unlocking the law of attraction.

21. Change your lifestyle

One way in which you can change your life is by making wise decisions about the things that make up your lifestyle.

22. Positive Mindset

An important part of unlocking the law of attraction is to have a positive mindset. It's not only enough to be happy, but also it’s important to feel content and grateful for what you

23. Avoid fighting with others

One of the most negative things you can do is fight with others. Having conflict with people produces a lot of stress and it's important to reduce this as much as possible.

24. Remove abusive language and negative thoughts.

Negative energy is one of the most difficult things to find peace with. Toxic people and their negative words can have a seriously damaging effect on your mental state, so it's important that you remove them from your life as much as possible.

One way to avoid negative energy is by stopping abusive language in your head. It's important that when someone does something wrong, we don't take it in and certainly don’t let that become part of our internal dialogue.

25. Find happiness in simple pleasures

It's easy to feel stressed when there are many demands from such toxic people and it can feel like you have to do everything for them. But the simplest things, such as taking a walk outside or enjoying a meal with friends are enough to bring peace back into your life.

Chapter 5: How Consciousness and Vibration Works

Conscious vibrations work in the spiritual realm. This means that the vibrations are not limited by time and space as they can transcend into other dimensions of reality.

We've heard the phrase we are what we eat, but what we think and how we feel is also important.

Negative thoughts can create negative vibrations that manifest into our reality. From this perspective, it's possible to experience a lower vibration by thinking the wrong things or paying attention to negativity around us.

The secret key of spirituality to Vibrate Higher is about removing the negative thoughts and feelings to get to a higher vibration. And so instead focus on the positive or pursue what you desire.

In this light, blocking negativity and focusing on positive vibes are two paths to manifesting a more fruitful outcome, rather than just following blindly like most of us do in our daily lives.

Therefore a conscious approach to our lives can help us to vibrate on a higher frequency and experience a more fulfilling life.

My spiritual awakening began when I started to consciously remove the negative thoughts that had been running through my mind, which caused me to become overwhelmed with negativity in my day-to-day living. By following this principle for our personal energy, we can achieve peace.

The Mind is a powerful thing and it can be a burden if we are not taking care of our spiritual self.

In order to create the life you want, make peace with your past, find solace in forgiveness, and focus on what is positive for your future.

To shape our thoughts, words, and actions to be more positive can help us get what we want in life. This is the Law of attraction - just as like attracts like.

So if you put out negative thoughts they will come back to you with even greater negativity; instead, put out positivity and it will attract all kinds of goodness into your life!

This is what is means to be conscious with our vibe, just as conscious with our thoughts, words and actions. We can energetically vibrate higher by releasing negative energy, which is the cause of all struggles in life

And so the secret is to catch it before it arises, as soon as you feel the negative energy coming on, you can let it go as soon as possible to avoid the effects.

Letting go of negative energy is a great way to Vibrate Higher and stay connected with your spiritual awareness!

Here are some tips for releasing negativity:

- Go outside where there is fresh air or take a bath in water - both allow us to clear our senses

- Meditate if we find ourselves feeling overwhelmed or stressed; this also helps release tension from the mind and body which alleviates feelings of stress

- Avoid listening to music that makes you feel bad about yourself because it will only limit the positive spin.

- Spend time with positive people -- those that make us laugh; inspire us without judgement, accepting to all.

A recent exposé revealed that our thoughts not only create our reality, but also have the power to change it.

Studies in thought science revealed that as we change our thoughts, we could alter the perception of reality.

This means that what you think about is more powerful than anything else in your life because it creates a vibration for which all things are now attuned to!

The law of attraction reveals this principle: "whatsoever thou shalt think, then so shall it be". If something bad happens and all you can do is only feel sorry for yourself or those around you who may have lost their job - well guess what? You will continue attracting negativity into your world with more loss.

We have free will in the sense that we attract our experiences but it is also true that we have a choice of which kind of experience - negative or positive-to elicit from any given situation.

High Vibration Vs. Low Vibration

When it comes to comparing vibrations, a high vibration is an experience or feeling of joy, peace and harmony. A low vibration would be one that generates fear, lack of self-worth and little sense of wellbeing in the individual experiencing it.

The exact distinctions between how low and high vibrations are experienced may vary from person to person.

We often use the law of attraction as a tool for how we create our reality in life but it is also true that there are other unseen energies such as spiritual awareness and ego, which can have a strong effect on our vibrations.

An individual may experience both high and low vibrations in any given day but the person's predominant vibration will be one or the other at any particular time.

A healthy life is about balance, so we cannot achieve this when all of our energies are focused solely on negative experiences, which manifest themselves as fear.

<u>List of low Vibration are:</u>

- fear

- anxiety

- stress

- guilt and shame.

<u>List of high Vibration are</u>:

- love, gratitude, kindness and acceptance.

For the majority of people who have experienced these positive emotions they will resonate with a higher vibration than those that feel low.

Here's a list of negative low vibe emotions and how they can be healed:

- Fear - The fear of the future, over analyzing, feeling anxious or powerless.

- Anxiety - Feeling overwhelmed by what could happen in the present moment. Constantly worrying and never being able to relax.

- Stress - A constant state of worry, which impacts all aspects of one's life

Here's a list of positive high vibe emotions and how to make them feel even better:

- Love - The unconditional love of oneself, the connection with others and the world.

- Gratitude - For everything that has happened in one's life as a result of what led up to now. Feeling thankful for all aspects of their past lives which have led into this moment.

Chapter 6: Evidence of Vibrational Energy

Higher Vibration What Does it Mean? Why is it important?

In Quantum Physics, everything has a vibration. For example an atom and molecule come together to make matter into other states, such as liquids, solids, and gas. This process is known as "quantum entanglement."

The evidence of Vibrational Energy is something we can see around us. It's the natural law of attraction that we know as "sympathetic resonance."

Vibrational Energy is a form of energy with vibrating atoms. There are different types and levels of vibration, which cause waves to be generated at various frequencies.

Higher Vibration comes from keeping an open mind about life in general and allowing yourself to tune into the natural law of attraction that we know as "sympathetic resonance."

Higher Vibration is about living with a sense of wonder, allowing you to be open and receptive. It's stepping outside the confines of what you have been told or led to believe must happen in your life and believe there are other possibilities for you because this world has sympathetic resonance means if you vibrate at a frequency that is in harmony with the universe, you will be rewarded for it.

Higher Vibration is about connecting to yourself and trusting your intuition because we all have an inner guidance system that can see our path before us and guide us through life if we allow ourselves to tune into it.

This means that everything and everyone-including you, has a vibration. And this includes your thoughts, which have their own frequency.

The great physicist Albert Einstein said vibration is the key to unlocking our universe's secrets and we can use vibration in order to get what we want.

For example, Vibrations can also be used in order to heal oneself or others by using healing sound vibrations which help modulate the energy field that surrounds us in an aura of positive charge.

Another example of evidence of vibrational energy is the fact that our cells are built up of molecules made of atoms that vibrate at a certain frequency.

And so, we must first understand and work on changing our vibration in order to change anything else so as to manifest what we want into being.

A practical example of this principle can be seen when tuning a guitar, for example. If you have a string that is too high in pitch and you want to bring it down, then all you need to do is shorten the length of the string by pressing on one end until there's less tension which will allow the other end of the string to vibrate at a lower frequency where we want it.

The frequency and the amplitude or intensity of that vibration determine what it is classified as-whether it's living, dead, spiritual, physical etc.

Everything has a vibrational level which reflects its state of being in this moment.

Imagine that life is a symphony or concert which, in itself, consists of an infinite number of different notes. Each note has its own vibration and the whole orchestra, each individual instrument playing their part-is all vibrating together to compose this grand composition we call life.

In the same way, we are all vibrating at different levels, some more intensely than others and it's up to us to tune in and find our own personal frequency.

<u>We have a choice of which vibration we want-the low or high</u>:

Our thoughts originate from that point of origin. We can either think about something negatively or positively; we're open to frequencies and yet also have the power to make real change possible. It is, therefore, from a conscious position that we must take action and tune into our personal frequency to get to our desired state.

How Vibrational Energy Works.

To fully understand how vibrations work, we need to first understand the concept of energy. Energy is everywhere and everything in this world; it's what drives our thoughts, feelings and actions.

When your mind forms a habit it is taking shape in not just your thinking but also as we know, habits also shape our real world.

It is the mind that first and foremost, shapes our world – which starts the connection.

So how does Vibrational Energy work? They are energies of different frequencies or vibrations as they were and they exist in both visible and invisible realms.

The invisible energies are more potent than the visible energies that we can see and feel.

Vibrations travel through space, air molecules and even our own bodies. Vibrational Energy is what makes up everything in this world. We owe it to ourselves to understand how they work so we may shape our lives by consciously tuning into them on a deeper level.

For example, if we want to be more creative then it is necessary for us to tune into the Vibrational Energy of creativity.

A person's vibration must increase before they can attain what they have set out in their life path or desired outcome.

It comes down to how much energy you are giving off and taking on throughout your day. The higher the vibrational energy, the more desirable your outcome and experience will be.

The better you are able to align with a higher vibrational energy vibration, the easier it is for you to create what it is that you want in life. It's not just about thinking positively or visualizing - those things can certainly help but there needs to be an alignment of Consciousness.

This perfect alignment of consciousness and vibration will help you to achieve what it is that you desire.

You must focus on the feeling of having accomplished your goal in order to maintain this vibration and tap into its energy.

For example when you have a gut feeling that you will meet a specific person, or find something that you've been looking for - keep the feeling of certainty in your mind.

Your mind is always working to bring your thoughts and feelings into reality.

If you feel like something is going to happen - it probably will!

The way that you can tap into the law of attraction is by aligning with a vibration that feels right for YOU. When you are vibrating higher, anything becomes possible because this energy helps others see what's in front. Your vibrations will magnetize what you want to come your way. This is because the law of attraction always works to bring your thoughts and feelings into reality. Your mind is always sending you signals or frequencies that will either maintain the same vibration as where you are or raise it.

Sometimes when we feel like something is going to happen, it actually does! This can be because we have already been thinking about it and sending out a frequency that aligns with this idea. When you think of things happening in your life, what do you focus comes into being?

It's time to clear the old and make space for new energy. The thoughts that have sustained you for so long might no longer be working well, or may not even serve your highest good anymore. It can help to find a more powerful perspective of yourself by reading spiritual books such as this to help you raise your vibration.

The law of attraction is a universal spiritual principle that states what we give out will always come back to us, so by being kind and loving toward others, or ourselves, not only do our vibrations shift closer to the high frequency but also attract more positive people in life who are on this same wavelength.

It's now up to you what you are going to give out into the world and how your life will turn out.

Be true to yourself, be real in everything that you do and believe only what is best for you. All it takes is a few small tweaks here and there such as taking care of oneself first, banishing negative thoughts from one's mind by letting go, and surrounding oneself with positivity to help create the life one desires.

When it comes to manifesting what you want, this is an essential part of the process!

In order to maintain an elevated vibration and make these things happen more often, all it takes is some practice.

Chapter 7: Signs of High Vibration

***How to know the signs of high vibration*?**

- When you are in a state of flow, it's unlikely that anything can stop the process.

- You would feel calm and content with your life.

- On the other hand, whenever you have a feeling of emptiness or loneliness, remember to focus on something more uplifting like the beautiful sunset outside for example!

The energy around someone who is in a state of high vibration is contagious!

Here are some examples:

- thankfulness

When you are thankful for everything in your life, you are recognizing the good that is already there.

- gratitude

Gratitude expands an individual's capacity to receive more of what they want from their spiritual path and their environment because it opens up a feeling of endless possibilities!

- Abundance mentality

When you have an abundance mindset, you see potential and possibility everywhere.

- appreciation

When we are grateful, it's easier to appreciate all the people in our lives who have been there for us no matter what!

- Avoid Drama

When vibrating higher it's clear avoidance from drama is necessary.

- Practice Self care

Those that vibrate higher understand the importance of self-care and put it first.

- Acceptance

Acceptance is the key to living in peace with whatever life throws your way because when you can accept, then you are free!

- Trusting thyself

When we trust ourselves we have a better understanding of our true power, which leads us to feel at home with who we are and what our destiny is.

- Learning to let go

When you can learn to let things go, life becomes much easier! You don't have any negative energy weighing on your mind or soul, which allows for the law of attraction to work wonders in your life!

- Feel mentally strong

This doesn't mean that you can't ever feel sad, frustrated or angry. But it does mean that when you do experience these emotions, they don't last for days and are short-lived which allows your mind to be free of clutter!

But also mentally resilient people have the ability to change their entire thought process and attitude within a few minutes!

- Content

When you are content, you have the ability to listen in a way that is non-judgmental and accepting. This means no matter what someone else says or does it doesn't affect your belief system!

Content people are also able to easily focus on one thing at a time. This means they are able to stay on-task.

Content people focus more on doing things for themselves than they do for other people. This includes their work and keeping things moving forwards.

- Emotional Balance

People with higher vibrational energy are also more emotionally balanced. They don't have the same consistency of highs and lows that someone with a lower vibration may experience.

This is because they feel in control of their life, rather than feeling out-of-control! It's all about being content vs. not being content.

Benefits of Higher Vibration

<u>Raising your vibrational energy can have a myriad of benefits. There are many advantages to this, which include:</u>

- Higher sense of self-worth and respect for oneself

- Less negative emotions such as anger or frustration (and less stress!)

- More positive outlook on life in general with a higher appreciation for what you have!

- More peace and contentment

- Greater health!

- personal freedom

Chapter 8: How to maintain a high Vibration?

You know the answer to this question. To raise your vibration, just keep doing what you're doing! It doesn't matter if it's reading inspirational books or practicing yoga; all of these activities will help lift and balance yourself in a way that is sustainable so long as you continue them each day. This also helps lead into living with more harmony and joy because when we are using those things which make us feel great over time - like exercise for example- then our body feels better too, making life easier overall!

When you are at peace, you can feel it tingling all over. It's so refreshing and relaxing to take a break from the hustle of everyday life and just sit in silence for awhile but then after meditating, we have to return back into our daily lives where there is always something going on like dealing with co-workers or family members or juggling ten things at once! I've come upon an interesting realization recently that many people may be feeling this drop off due to being too busy trying not only maintain their work responsibilities but also sustain that higher level of consciousness through every moment. Let's try some mindfulness techniques such as taking breaks throughout your day by listening closely when someone speaks while staying engaged even if they're silent afterwards

Today, I want to talk about what you're going through. We live in the physical realm and there are many challenges. There is duality, chaotic energy of others, and also the energy that has been here for thousands of years on earth... And now we have a chance to anchor it because as humans we can change this paradigm together!

Once we realize that there is a difference between heavy energy and negative thoughts, it becomes easier to respond in the right way.

Be mindful. If you're feeling heavy energy and start judging yourself, your ego-mind spirals out of control - You say things like "I' want to see better improvements." Then this becomes what you are creating but if you pause and notice "I'm feeling some heavy energy," then don't take it on as a reflection of who you are – Just let it pass.

Your awareness of your feelings beyond love, light and joy is important. You can then release these other emotions that have been coming up in you or are from the collective consciousness.
Once you know this about yourself, it's a good idea to allow them to move through rather than latching onto them each time they come around.

Maintaining a high vibration is an important part of maintaining the higher levels of vibration that you're tuning into, involves awareness and being able to shift when old patterns, beliefs or densities kick in. Recognize and be aware that when low energy appears - like feeling your mood drop off- it's not a reflection on who you are authentically but rather something else entirely; have awareness about what needs to happen next so as long as we maintain our intention for change, there will always be opportunities within us waiting for us to see them

It is a sure-fire way to lower your vibration if you are scrolling through social media. Take time out in nature or meditation for some refreshment and resetting of the mind, body, and soul.

It's natural to feel off sometimes, so do what you need to shift your energy. Simply recognize that it is not a reflection of your vibrational state for you to be feeling less than amazing! Pay attention the information and self-talk that is currently being ingested. Have been scrolling through Facebook feed? That will lower your vibration fast-- get out in nature today instead.

Are you feeding high vibration into your body? Are you eating raw fruits and vegetables filled with life force energy or are you eating heavily processed food and meat-filled that's lowering your field and allowing yourself to become susceptible to negativity. Is someone else latching onto you energetically with cords? Are you letting someone else drain your energy so that it feels exhausting, worn out, and irritable? Ask your inner self what it is and then to cut the cord draining you.

The idea of maintaining your vibration is flawed because you cannot stay the same. In this world we live in, there's no standing still. Change is a constant; you may have heard the phrase 'If you're not growing, then you're dying.' While it might sound harsh on an energy level--it's true that if you are not actively rising your own vibration-your frequency will decline.

In each moment of your life, you have the opportunity to choose love. This includes moments where you feel challenged. If you are weighed down by negativity, recognize that at this moment in time your job is to shift gears and take a different path forward.

Return to Love

The present moment is your opportunity to choose love, and light up your being. This includes the moments where you feel challenged. If you're feeling weighed down by negativity, recognize that in those moments it's time to shift away from them

Imagine being surrounded by a giant bubble of light. It's so bright that you can't see anything else in the room, but it doesn't feel uncomfortable or overwhelming because it is coming from your heart and radiating outward to encompass everything around you with warmth and love.

Now close your eyes--the darkness makes this experience much more intense as colors swirl all around like brightly flashing strobe lights at an insane dance party! You are floating on water; it feels cool against your skin even though there is not any liquid nearby. The sound surrounds you: waves lapping against each other and onto shore...you're getting closer to something wonderful-a place where time slows down, thoughts still their chatter for just a moment, a special space where worries cease if they are not teaching you something.

You're never alone. You have an unlimited number of helpers that are waiting for you to call them in when needed. Imagine a dial with the numbers 1-10 on it and turn up your level of light this way, so you can shine brighter, more radiantly and open yourself up to love even more than before!

It's okay to take a day off

You are a spiritual being who is evolving and this process can be full of peaks and valleys. Stand in your authentic light, even if you have an off day every now and then. Trust that it's OK to feel energetic at times or down at other moments; neither one means anything about failure.

When you can objectively view reality as a temporary experience of low vibrations, then it is no longer an obstacle for us. We take back our power from the situation and we are not lowered down in vibration because of that issue. Whenever possible, shift your energy towards love, growth and raising your frequency to be higher than before!

Claim Your Power

To keep your energy high, instead of being weighed down by a challenge or feeling low and heavy take action. Go for an invigorating hike, work out in the gym, do some push-ups around your living room. Do what you need to shift-up.

You cannot control how others feel or act, but you can set your own mood and energy to whatever level that is most comfortable for yourself. Listen carefully to what's bugging the other person? Find a way to be supportive while still maintaining some self-assurance of who you are.

The more you raise your vibration and align with your full light, the more open to new levels of abundance, clarity, certainty and self-love. This is how not only do you step into fulfilment in life but also as a way-shower for humanity. Step into this role by coming together with others who are committed to positive change!

You were not put on this earth to hide your light and keep up the status quo. You are an authentic spiritual being in physical form who can thrive and prosper by choosing love, joy, peace with yourself while shining brighter than ever before!

You are never too high. I can feel it in my bones and every fibre of being, that there is always a higher level for us to reach together.

Once a thought has been formed it now vibrates into a physical form, such as a habit or action and this is what we call something is manifested. This is a clear key take-away when assessing your daily vibrations.

Chapter 9: Raising your vibrational energy

You've probably noticed by now how having certain kinds of thoughts occupies differing frequencies, with more highly-vibrating ones yielding positive outcomes whereas those operating at slower rates tend towards negatives. With this understanding in hand, if there's something specific that one wants for their life or future self then increasing his/her own vibrations is key - focus all energies on these desired realities so they can come about!

The vibrational frequencies of shame and guilt can be charted from the lowest level to enlightenment at the highest point. The chart is split into two sections, with one containing adverse effects that are caused by lower vibratory frequency levels while in contrast on the other side rests a positive impact created by higher vibrational frequencies.

Certain frequencies are more effective than others in various situations. Going from a lower vibration to higher one is not merely about quickly switching; you have to go through the transition period. However, if you're at high vibrational frequency by how much energy feel within and are self-aware of your thoughts then it will be easier for the shift in consciousness.

The higher your vibrational frequency, the better you are at connecting with your spiritual self. Most people fall somewhere on a spectrum of various levels of vibration and rarely remain completely in one place for long periods of time. Increasing our vibration is thus identifying aspects we're improving upon as well as those that need work."

Increasing your vibrational frequency means that with each and every moment that passes; produces rumbling butterflies of energy which will allow us to connect.

Why Is It Important To Raise Your Vibration?

Stress, fear and anxiety vibrate at a lower frequency than happiness or joy does which makes us less equipped physically because it lowers our defences against illness but as this passage shows it also affects morale with negative emotions like sadness affecting self-esteem while positive ones such as humor can boost them.

It has been studied that negative emotions and feelings such as anxiety, fear and stress have been proven to reduce the immune system, which is our internal warrior for fighting off illness within the body.

Furthermore, on an energetic understanding, these negative emotions also block heart chakra; disconnecting us from ourselves.

Most of our day is driven by unconscious mind with built-in behavior patterns that control how much energy we have in any given moment. When we're in a lower vibrational state of fear, stress or anxiety - like when it's late at night after being up all day long because you've been under pressure (not your best self) – then there's really no hope for productivity whatsoever!

Emotions can be scientifically shown to make people more susceptible to sicknesses as they suppress their natural defences against them. It has been scientifically proven that this will cause negative effects on several other aspects of health such as cognitive function (memory), depressive symptoms, cardiovascular disease risk factors--even mortality rate!

The immune system protects against infection but due to various environmental stresses, we see more people with chronic diseases than ever before leaving many feeling helpless about their own illnesses.

Your life feels closed off and driven by out-dated old thoughts. You may be hugging yourself, crossing your arms as the whole body goes into protection 'fear mode' in fear of what is going on around you.

Your thoughts and perceptions are the primary cause of illness today. Perception can change everything – you, your world, your biology, energy levels, and vibration. The main reason we need to increase our vibration is because epigenetic science now shows that ills created by the mind can cause long term effects. The mind controls every aspect of one's life from perception which changes what they see in their world until it influences how they behave physically (elevated or lowered) as well as biologically (energy level).

Ways To Raise Your Vibration

Whenever we want to get more in tune with our energy, there are many ways that can be done. Sometimes the easiest way is by sitting down and meditating or getting somewhere quiet--which might not always work out when it comes time for us to do so.

Sitting still and trying to find some peace of mind could seem like a daunting task sometimes but don't stress!

Here's some detailed tips on how you can raise your vibration right now:

1. Put out high-frequency energy

The higher the frequency, the more aligned you are with truth. This is based on love and connection- a high vibration includes gratitude, appreciation of yourself and others without attached expectations or need for control; openness to opportunities in life that come your way; presence which means being fully conscious/aware during each moment in our lives so we can live it authentically instead of living through outside distractions such as media overload or social comparisons. Acceptance (of self first) translates into acceptance of those around us who may behave differently than what society deems normal- compassion requires understanding another person's perspective before judging them harshly while encouraging personal growth. Trusting oneself also fosters faith - I surrender my fears because they don't serve me any longer when faced with new challenges.

The more you approach life with this positive energy, you raise your overall frequency (because it's the truth of the higher law) and so start to experience more miracles. You start to have more synchronicities in life, shifts into a better mindset or way of being that really resonates with just how we are all supposed to be living our lives.

Live with love. Find peace within yourself and be open to new ideas and people. Follow your passions; create something beautiful, both inwardly as well as outwardly - enriching not only those around you but also the world in which we live!

Give love what-ever you can, sometimes it's a hug and other times somebody is there to listen. See the good in situations; not all things are bad. Speak out if you're scared or upset with someone else - say what needs to be said instead of holding it in like I did for so long! Trust yourself as much as you trust others, even when they let us down over and over again but we still come back for more anyway because that little glimmer of hope has never left our hearts since this journey began way back then...

2. Engage with life in a childlike way!

Embrace your childlike nature! The world is yours to explore and experience; be adventurous, curious, open-minded. Be imaginative and creative in every aspect of life! Don't let society hold you back from exploring the wonders that exist outside - go on a spontaneous adventure today or climb trees with friends while having fun!!! Explore new things, get dirty when needed. Adventure awaits!!

3. Give to another without expecting anything in return

You know what makes you feel good? Giving to others. When we give to others selflessly or when we do something kind for someone else, by the beautifully designed nature of man's mind, WE are naturally made joyful too. We have been blessed with this ability and it is a great gift that make people happy in return - not just ourselves but those who receive from us as well!

Giving back can be an incredible way to lift your mood because it allows you the opportunity to share true kindness without expecting anything in return except happiness which multiplies exponentially greater than any sum of money could ever buy off-hand

You don't need to sacrifice your energy, health and wellbeing just for the sake of making others happy. Do not give up because you feel guilty or pressured into giving something away- that would be a low vibrational act. Never give out of obligation or pressure - only do so when it comes from a place of love!

4. Practice present moment awareness

Becoming aware of your thoughts is not letting them run the show, it's being more conscious about what you do, say and think. We all have tendencies that get us when we are not paying attention to them; they sort of just kick in and take over for a while. For example if you tend to be angry often but don't become consciously aware of it then naturally react with anger every time something comes up which triggers this response within yourself -but once becoming mindful or at least somewhat attentive-you can change your reaction into one more effective and positive instead!

By reframing your mindset and focusing on praising instead of criticizing, appreciating instead of complaining, forgiving instead of blaming, accepting in stead of resenting you can enjoy life more. Practicing mindfulness is key to living each day mindfully; this does not just mean paying attention to yourself but also being alert and focused while still responding appropriately with awareness during the present moment around you. Do things both intentionally and consciously with intention instead of blindly following a preset mode or routine—to live fully!

5. Change your language

Pause for a moment and take some time to really assess your words. It is not enough to just use words, pay attention to the nature of your language.

Would you like to hear yourself during a normal conversation? Does it sound positive and empowering or do you feel self-conscious when speaking this way because society has imposed these standards on how we should act in public space for centuries now?" Your tone matters too; does your voice reflect what you want people to associate with who "YOU" are inside as opposed as outside forces dictating our behavior based off social values that have been set by cultural norms so long ago."

You might be surprised to know that we have certain tendencies without realizing it, and one of them is how we speak. And while this may seem like a small thing at first glance, the way you express yourself can say more about your personality than anything else in communication with others!

I think one of the things that are hard for people to realize is how much their voice and expression can shape who they become. It's not just about what you say, it's also about how you say it: your tone, pace, volume - these all have an impact on the way listeners perceive us.

Again we have certain tendencies, which sort of happen without us even realizing it. And among them is our way with words-the ways in which we speak and express ourselves; this too separates each person from another like a key difference between two pieces of art or writing styles would do so as well!

I'm going to have a conversation with my friend and record it. I am not judging myself, but instead observing the nature of my language. Words you use, tone of voice, body language etc., You can also do this in your regular environment through constant awareness and observation (like #4), or have a friend pay attention to you point out tendencies

6. Become conscious of your thoughts.

Thoughts are the single most important thing you have. They shape your reality, and any given thought can change what happens to you in a day or more than that!

It's easy to think that way when you're in the face of adversity. But what about this? Next time a negative thought shows up in your head, take some time to acknowledge it and thank it for showing up so you can turn things around for the positive.

7. Be conscious of the foods you eat.

Eating is a sensory experience. The way you feel after eating certain foods differs from one person to the next, and some people may be sensitive or have allergies to these items that other individuals are not affected by at all. Eating healthy organic produce results in feeling high vibrations throughout your body because of how nature intended food should taste; it makes most sense for each individual to pay attention on how their own bodies react when consuming different types of foods so they can then make educated decisions about what works best for them personally rather than relying solely on social norms.

8. Meditation

Meditation is a way to find peace and happiness in ourselves by coming inward, recognizing we are all that we need. It involves clearing negative energy and the chaos often found within our minds. We can bring ourselves into a greater state of flow and higher vibration through meditation because it allows us to let go of so much that no longer serves us.

Sit down for five to ten minutes. Then move into focusing on your breath, continually bringing attention back to it when you notice your mind wandering in the present moment. Once your attention has been fully captured by the breath, use it is a distraction-free zone where thoughts are not allowed in without permission.

The process of affirmation is a powerful tool. Affirmations are statements that you recite to yourself in order to help ground and affirm your thoughts, desires, goals or intentions while also giving them more energy than regular thinking would do. For example: "I am light," "I am vibrating at higher frequencies" or “ I have everything I need within myself” can all be used as affirmations for grounding oneself into practice and affirming the self with love when desired.

9. Music

Listening to upbeat music may be the easiest way to raise your frequency and quickly. Sound has a powerful effect on humans as sound is literally vibrations, and listening to certain frequencies will help you elevate your vibe.

Studies have been done to prove that music can really change your mood and even go as far as acting a type of therapy not only to help boost your mood but also relieve stress. The great thing is that music is available all the time! So next time you're feeling down, put on your favorite playlist and feel the benefits sound healing through music in seconds.

10. Aromatherapy

Aromatherapy is a healing technique used for centuries, which uses scents (typically essential oils) to promote health and well-being. Certain smells cause people to experience different emotions because they influence the brain - specifically, they stimulate an area of the brain called "limbic system" that controls behavior, emotion, motivation and memory as we know it today.

You can use different scents to raise your vibration. For example, lavender which is a popular scent for relaxation and relieving stress. Eucalyptus, chamomile, and frankincense are also great calming scents. Scents like peppermint or citrus (orange, grapefruit) can help as they offer mood-supporting uplifting vibes too!

Oils can be used in many different ways, such as diffused directly on the skin or added to water and inhaled via steam.

Oil is a liquid and sometimes stronger than others. Some oils have very specific uses, so it's important to understand the oil you are working with. Oils can be diffused, added to carrier oils like sweet almond oil or jojoba oil (most essential oils in their pure state are too concentrated for direct application on skin), applied directly on skin (mostly behind ears or on wrists), added water and sprayed into air, or they may also be used by adding them to boiling water from which steam will then inhale via distance of course.

You can get many of the same benefits as aromatherapy by burning incense or candles (which are also great for setting a room's mood and increasing vibrational energy)!

11. Movement

Moving your body has a positive vibrational effect.

Move your body through exercise, massage, or yoga. different movements, such as walks in nature or dancing have their own unique vibrational quality.

Move promotes the release of endorphins. Endorphins are the brain's natural painkiller, and also act to lift your mood which will inspire you to keep moving in a positive way.

These exercises help you reach higher vibrational frequencies, which is why they are very healthy for the body mind complex (BMC).

It has been proven that exercise can prevent disease and illness, as well as contribute to someone living a longer life. It loosens your joints, expands your lungs, and improves circulation in the blood and lymphatic system. This not only helps with muscle building but helps with toxin removal from the immune system too. Exercise sends all of this good energy out into the world around you and attracts more of it back to you automatically, which is how movement can heal you.

Along with mood enhancing natural chemicals such as endorphins during movement of exercise the body also releases chemically a hormone called Oxytocin. This hormone is actually scientifically proven to make you happier and feel good. It has also been linked to improving fertility in women, increasing trust between people (if you're working out with someone) and reduces anxiety and fear.

In fact, there are no negatives that come from exercise except getting the right diagnosis on what your body can handle which will be discussed later on how to do exactly this.

The best part about vibrating higher daily through exercise is that it costs you absolutely nothing but time!!

Finally, the endorphins, serotonin, and dopamine that we all know about are also released during a workout session. These chemicals make you feel great and actually kill the feelings of pain in your body as well!!!

The reason why i put this together is because exercise is really important for us to be able to vibrate higher every day. In fact, if you're not exercising now then you should get going right away! If it's easier for you to start walking outside than on a treadmill or elliptical then do that and work your way up from there. Start small, but start today!

Overall advantages of vibrating higher through exercise include: increased brain power, better circulation (helps remove toxins), staying strong makes getting older less scary since our bodies stay healthier longer without disease, and better adapted to overcoming stress.

This will also reduce the activity of hormones like adrenalin and cortisol, in your body, which make you feel less stressed and anxious all the time. And even if you're a full-time employee or parent—or both!—that's not necessarily an excuse to ignore this critical aspect of your life. As much as it is important to de stress and take care of yourself from the inside out, so is strengthening your body and making sure that it feels good at the end of every day.

The main reason I love exercise is the immediate gratification I get from completing a workout. Those positive feelings make me want to do more and help push me toward my long-term goals. Plus, exercising releases happy hormones like serotonin which help us sleep better and help increased productivity the next day which cycles the feel-good cycle back around even more.

Finally: exercising releases, the brain chemicals that make you feel good and happy! That means better sleep and an improved mood the next day for a happier, healthier you. And who doesn't want to be happy?

Building a fitness routine is as easy or hard as you make it out to be. It really takes being conscious of your current fitness level and working up from there. Even if this simply means walking around the block three times a week instead of driving to work every morning. The important thing is just getting started! Changing your lifestyle can be hard enough, why not combine two things you love into one?

12. Maintain a daily routine

A daily routine is a great way to start living healthier.

I always start my morning routine with five minutes of silent meditation. This helps me clear my mind for the day ahead, followed by a delicious coffee. Having this focus really helps me to disconnect and find time for myself before I actually start planning my day.

Getting up early to plan your day ahead is a great way to start living healthier. You'll have more time during the day to focus on your health goals and come up with creative ways to fit exercise into your schedule. Start an evening meditation practice or write in a journal before you go to bed every night. This will help you slow down and ground yourself each day so you're less likely to make unhealthy decisions when it's difficult to think clearly, such as when you're hungry or tired.

A schedule helps you stay on top of your work, family and yourself. If you're worried that your routine might get monotonous, find different ways to keep it interesting. Take a cooking class or join a gym with an exercise variety that interests you.

You can even make small changes for big results. Maybe switching out soda for water is easier than giving up dairy entirely. Or using the stairs instead of the elevator is easier than working out in the gym if you have a busy schedule.

To maintain a daily habit of increased vibration, find one or two things that make you happier and go from there. Try to incorporate things into your life, which can help you feel better about yourself. This can be a step toward the ultimate goal of feeling happy and creating a higher vibration for your life on a daily basis.

It's true that what you focus on expands, meaning that if you're unhappy or constantly worrying about things, they'll only expand and get bigger. When you change your thinking to happier thoughts, those situations in your life will begin to improve as well.

In order to vibrate higher each day, practice gratitude every day. Being grateful for the positive things in your life allows positive energy flow into your world and helps sel-love grows naturally from within. If you aren't used to being grateful yet however, it might seem awkward at first, but keep trying until feels right.

I know we hear about gratitude all the time these days, so I want to point towards moments that bring you inner joy. Do things that can immediately uplift your vibrational energy in the day. What brings you inner joy is different from person to person, but I encourage you to find out what brings you the most pleasure. One thing that has always brought me good energy is when I make food for my family and friends. It puts love into the cooking process, which makes it an activity with high vibrational energy flow. Something about getting all of our favorite flavors in one dish just seems so indulgent and exciting!

Eventually, your vibration is going to increase naturally, making you feel more successful in every area of your life.

13. Declutter

Very little is spoken about how clutter is low-vibe and I want to bring the clutter you have both inside your home and your mind to your attention. Your home is the first place to look at because it usually gives us more anxiety than any other circumstance. Are you surrounded by piles of papers, plastic containers or just random stuff that's been in your house for too long? Imagine these things are toxic, causing physical harm and imbalancing your mood and energy levels. Throw away all that excess stuff and clean out your home from top to bottom. You don't need to live like a minimalist but if you have some space issues in your apartment or house, take a day off work and get rid of ALL the clutter! It'll make cleaning so much easier as well. Be ruthless!

In this same way, think of the inner clutter deep within ourselves. There's likely no physical clutter in our minds but there is a lot of excess energy; fear, frustration, anger. These are toxic feelings that we can never get rid of on our own so we need an expert to help us cleanout. Also, think about the people closest to you who love you so dearly and respect you ... but are they creating any kind of negative energy to you, for themselves or others?

This process doesn't need to be so challenging, it should feel more like a game and it should be fun! Think of each item you have accumulated and do not need any more, find a good place for it, donate it to a local charity shop or a friend in need.

14. Explore nature

I know we've spoken about this previously, but to explore the natural beauty of mother earth will make you feel incredible. It's almost as if nature was created for us to experience, and it has so many hidden pleasures that can be discovered for a lifetime of joy!

For example, you could stand under a tree, in a rain shower with your eyes closed, and really focus on how much positive energy you are receiving from being outdoors, listening to the raindrops falling against the leaves or the wind whistling loudly. Let yourself just 'be' without any thought whatsoever... allow yourself to drift away into this magical place as if nothing else existed but you and your inner peace.

Breathe fresh air. And feel the sunshine on your skin, and the heat at your feet. Try it right now. Just stop reading and stand up from your computer. Walk onto a balcony, or even outside if the weather permits (it's summer in Australia right now, so go find some fresh air!)

When you breathe deeply and really concentrate on living in the moment, there is no room for ‘negative' thoughts – they just don't exist anymore! Our mind has power over our body and therefore how we feel.

Try to achieve this state of being as often as possible because you will feel happier than you ever thought possible once you get into a daily routine of cleansing your mind with pure thoughts rather than negative ones! The more time spent thinking of positive energy sources like these will help keep your vibrations high throughout the day.

15. Smiling and laughing

It has been scientifically proven that, even if you fake a smile, or laugh, your body will release endorphins in to the blood stream causing you to really feel happy! Your vibrations are sure to be high whilst you can still remember how to laugh and be genuine with it!

Just think of all of the people around the world who laugh and smile at nothing just for a rush. They don't realise that they are actually creating their own batch of positive vibes and feeling amazing as a result.

So, if you feel unhappy or stressed then even faking a smile will help your mind to finally relax and set new thoughts into motion.

Studies show, laughing helps the immune system get strong and if you are laughing in real life then even better!

Some people find it hard to laugh alone so watch your favourite funny movie or show, buy a stand-up DVD and have a night in with friends. As long as you can smile, at least you will be pleased with yourself for trying something new; this will set off more positive vibrations into the air.

Or simply just look at pictures of dogs on Facebook and go 'Awwwww' or look at gifs featuring kittens (google them!) The Internet is here to help us all make ourselves feel happier... there's no harm in that! Even if the pictures/gifs don't manage to put a smile on your face, just reading what they are about.

16. Community

Human beings need community; the only creature that doesn't is a hermit on an island (possibly). It is human nature to seek out one another and interact, whether it is for support, friendship or romantic relationships. We are social animals and as humans we should feel comfortable around others especially if we know them well.

Keeping in touch with friends does not necessarily mean you have to be face-to-face; you can talk regularly over the phone or send regular messages to your close ones using social media such as Facebook or Twitter. These actions will create positive vibes because you will get the feeling of satisfaction just by knowing that you are in contact with people who care about you.

But find a group of people that lift you up and not drag you down (not everybody has the same intention). Surround yourself with people who are positive thinkers and perhaps even those who practice meditation to stay in the present moment.

With a conscious effort, you can create a group of friends that will be good for your spiritual growth as well as your mental happiness. It is also important to remember that there are many different types of friendships so do not pin point someone just by one label being their friend or acquaintance. You can have many acquaintances but only a few true-blue friends who will stick with you through thick and thin without letting emotions dictate their actions when it comes to seeing or talking to you. It is best advised that once you have found such wonderful friends, appreciate them more than anyone else because they see past all the BS.

Your environment will either lift you up or it will bring you down. If you are residing in an area that is filled with negativity, it would be best to move out of the negative energy and into a more positive environment where there are people who can help make your life simpler by holding you accountable when it comes to the things you want to achieve while also being around people that have the same goals as yourself. You do not need money to vibrate higher every day but if you're trying to become a better person spiritually, mentally and physically...it does not hurt at all..your surroundings definitely affect your personal growth so choose wisely!

Remember, everything is energy! Your thoughts and our emotions produce certain energies depending upon how we feel about something. When someone gives off negative vibes they most certainly have zero self-respect or love for others, and that's your time to leave.

17. Journal

Keeping a notebook to write down your thoughts is very therapeutic. It's always a good idea, to be honest with yourself so you can have a better understanding of how you perceive situations and why.

I get a lot of mental clarity from just sitting down with a nice cup of tea and journaling.

Keep a daily record. From time to time I like to look back on these things and see if anything has changed, if so, then maybe there is something I'm doing wrong.

Being honest with yourself and taking responsibility for your actions is the first step in your emotional growth. That's why it's important to keep a daily record because what we're really looking for is ourselves through emotions and daily happenings! Remember this when you begin writing down everything that happens throughout the day because there will be days where nothing seems to be going right at all but that's okay because life brings us experiences that cover up other experiences as well as teach us different lessons along the way.

If you feel the urge to confront people that are hurting you, this can help.

Sometimes this task is hard but it's worth the hassle, after all, it will allow you to cross paths with new opportunities because once people know that they cannot use someone else for their personal gain, they move on!

<u>If you want to increase your vibrational energy then use the following journal prompts</u>:

1. What am I grateful for right now?

2. How can I feel better about myself today?

3. Who do I appreciate in my life?

4. What is the best thing that has happened to me today? Identify one joyous occurrence and write it down, stay happy!

5. When was the last time I felt truly good about a person or place, what made it so special? Think of all the details that made you feel that way then think of how to remind yourself of this memory anytime you want to experience it again. This

helps us to understand from where some memories come from as well as live in the moment enough to remember them when they happen.

6. What is the biggest lesson I have learned today?

7. Whom could I help today by giving of my time, money or love?

8. How can I better nurture myself in some way that would benefit me and others around me? By making yourself a priority you resonate to your greatest potential and clearly see how taking care of yourself allows to be of service, this is how we truly vibrate higher!

9. When was the last time I just laughed out loud for no reason at all? Make sure you laugh on purpose in a positive way regularly because it helps with emotional healing from past experiences, joyful living and expands our awareness about what other possibilities are really out there.

18. Affirmations

Following on from daily journaling to vibrate higher daily it is also very useful to use affirmations. An affirmation is a positive statement spoken with emotion and the intention of changing things for the good, similar in some ways to prayer.

often when we feel in a state of low vibrational energy we tend to get stuck in our ways perhaps. That's where affirmations can really help shift things quicker.

However, they are an easy and powerful way to start vibrating higher whilst living in the here and now.

<u>Here is a shortlist of examples to get you started in your daily practice</u>:

I love myself and I am grateful for all that I have. Today, I choose happiness. Today is going to be glorious! Every day in every way it's getting better and better!

It's actually fairly important not to overdo this kind of work as otherwise, it becomes compulsive thinking so just use them on those days when you feel like you really want to hear it.

My life already has what I need. My life already has everything I need right now at this moment, so instead of focusing on what's missing or worrying about something not happening for me, I will focus my energy on feeling good about where I am at this present moment.

19. Visualization

Visualisation is the process use of using your mind to see and create your image, idea, goals and or thoughts or dreams as already having happened.

An easier way to approach this is to cut out images from magazines, newspapers or print images off and stick them up on a wall. Here, you can have several types of images/visualisation boards in each room of your home.

Additionally, you may add some text around them or targets/goals.

Seeing this visualization board each day will help you to see what you are aiming for every day and focus your mind on these things, which lift your energy to see the positive than getting caught into the old pattern of negative, thinking.

See the dream or image as already accomplished. This helps to lift your vibration and feel a sense of joy at the same time.

When you are happy with this visualization board, start adding other boards around your home to focus your mind on something positive new each day.

This can be anything from starting a business, making money online, completing an assignment for work or school, reconnecting with someone special in your life... Whatever makes you feel good! So long as it lifts your energy.

Repeat this step until you have enough boards across all rooms in your house/apartment or even just one room if it is small and doesn't take up too much space!

20. Focus on feeling good

This is where the technique of meditation will help to be more present and conscious of your everyday thoughts.

Meditation will help to center your focus to only good thoughts, positive thinking and the energy you wish for yourself. This in return helps you feel good about yourself and it shows. The more you feel good about yourself, the higher vibration you are on and attracting more of that feeling instead of what used to represent a low vibration. Positive thinking is key!

You can also visit any Buddhist temple or monastery (even if its just to ask questions!) They have been doing this for over thousands of years. They live by the philosophy "Be Happy Now".

The Buddhists meditate daily using mantras, which create a high vibrational state with their mind/spirit every day.

So being aware of your thoughts and focusing your energy on what you want rather than a low-vibe need, will help to manifest your desires.

Prayer is another way (which I personally do every night before bed) Ask to be lifted higher and be grateful for what you have already. Be thankful for where you're at in life and for what's coming into your life.

21. Clear your Subconscious

Did you know your subconscious mind is listening to every word you say? It is listening and reacting to everything you do. If your subconscious mind hears something enough times it will begin to believe that this is the type of life it must follow. When you program your subconscious with positive affirmations it will not only understand that this is what you want but also vibrate higher thereby allowing those things to come easily into view and manifest more quickly in your reality. Your subconscious does not differentiate between being spiritual or mundane; it just accepts the information as a command, so re-programming yourself on a daily basis can have positive effects in all areas of your life. The biggest mistake most make when using affirmative thoughts is that they use mirror language, "I am bad" vs I feel good.

Using Technology to Balance and Raise your Vibration

There are many devices you can use these days to help lift our energy. Especially, if you spend a lot of time online each day.

Find apps that can help you switch off like mindfulness apps that help to focus your energy on your vibe when feeling low. Perhaps place reminders throughout your day for certain self-care check-ins.

But more importantly, it's good to switch off from the digital as much as possible.

Unplug from the matrix

Take a break from your phones and spend more time with friends and family offline. Your energy will thrive when you unplug from the matrix of online social media. Not only that, but it's also a great way to reconnect with people on a deeper level.

The change in life is happening now! This generation has discovered something that has been known by ancient cultures who lived healthily and vibrantly for hundreds, maybe thousands of years before us; we are all one. We can feel good about ourselves just by thinking good thoughts:)

Remember there is no right or wrong vibration; what one person may see as negative could be seen as positive.

Chapter 10: Habits That Are Lowering Your Vibration

This list could go on and on! But for now, I just wanted to give you a few key examples of habits that will actually lower your vibration rather than raise it. This is by no means a full or comprehensive list; this is purely for examples.

Here's a quick introduction list of habits that lower your vibration and should be avoided:

1. Watching too much TV lowers your vibration as you are bombarded with subconscious fear propaganda and negative social conditioning. Becoming exhausted also lowers your vibration as your dreaming state becomes less lucid and asleep which keeps you from entering deeper trance states where more realizations can become clearer to you.

2. Drinking alcohol lowers your vibration by suppressing deeper meditation, lowering your frequency of thought and keeping your conscious mind asleep or more distracted so it can't become aware of the true nature of reality and your connection to Source. Alcohol is filled with poison! You will never be as productive and switched on the next if you were fresh rather than intoxicated.

3. Being around angry people, those who complain often and those who belittle or mock others all lower one's own frequency as negativity is contagious!

4. Eating foods that have been laced with pesticides, GMOs, hormones or other unnatural chemicals also causes a person's energy fields to drop drastically causing people not only to feel drained but also to think less which

5. Negativity

This is one that we all easily fall into, studies suggest that on average the negative thoughts we have per day outnumber the positive ones by at least five times! In reality, this number is probably a lot higher for those who think for themselves and are aware of their own potential.

What is negative thinking? It's basically anything that keeps you stuck in place; not allowing energy to flow and progress. This includes fear; worry, doubt, anger, resentfulness as well as any other emotionally charged thought patterns.

For example: If you wake up in the morning and tell yourself " I have no money now so I can't go out tonight!" This would be considered a negative thought because it discourages your conscious mind from accessing your potential abundance, which could eventually lead to you manifesting more money than just for the evening. The fact that we believe thoughts like this to be true is why so many people live in short-term thinking.

"I can't afford that yet, so I won't get it!" This type of thinking creates a separation between our conscious thoughts and our highest potential; the feeling that we're here to have fun while still working hard towards achieving abundant living.

Negativity does not have to be viewed as a negative term, however! It's all about how you look at things, which will dictate whether there is negativity or positive affirmations coming from your mouth.

For example: Instead of saying " I don't want this anymore, I'm sick of this situation!" One could say " Oh well, time for change! This isn't what I wanted but now, it's time to create a new reality!" This way you are still not dwelling on the negative and see it as an opportunity for change rather than something that has to be suffered through.

These types of tools will help you to lower your own negativity so that more positive thoughts can flow freely.

Negativity can also come from friends, family, co-workers and your job. If anything is bringing you down and really affecting you, then you must address it. Too many times we have been told you "grind it out", and "have grit", but honestly, some people, someplace and often employers are not worth it.

Remember; on average people spend more time at work than they do with their own families. If you're in a situation that is draining your energy or only creates low paying jobs for you then it's time to pull the cord and either find something better, change your attitude or move out of town!

It is often advised to pay attention to the number of days you stay home sick, or how many times a year you are in some kind of accident.

If there is an abnormally high amount then you probably are working in an energy-draining environment that needs to be changed. While it's good to work hard and have grit, it's also important not to forget your own well being as well. No money or title will ever be worth the toll neglecting your spiritual health will take on yourself physically, mentally and emotionally!

Using bad language

The words we use as well as our tone of speech can make us vibrate to different levels.

For example, being overly negative will literally lower your vibration making you feel drained and exhausted. This is why it's important to be aware of the words you are using because they really will affect how others see you and how you feel about yourself. If someone tells themselves " I'm always sick" then that's what their subconscious mind believes! Whenever an ailment comes up count how many days in a row they have been feeling under the weather, if there are more than three or four then this person needs to evaluate their own mental health versus taking medicine all day long.

Doing things that go against your values

Doing things which go against your values will lower your vibration because you're not being true to yourself. This can be living in a way that's unhealthy for you, ignoring family and friends whom care about you or anything else that just simply does not feel right.

To attract positive energy into your life it's important to first release the negative; don't fall victim to letting others pick up on what they see as flaws within yourself!

For example, If you continuously get angry every time someone annoys you at work then this low level of vibration is possible being felt by so many people all around you, not only creating a worse attitude from the rest of the staff but also drawing more negativity towards you.

This is why it's important to see where your low levels of vibrations are coming from and make the necessary changes so you can begin flowing with more positive energy.

Talking to Yourself

One thing many people will do when talking to others is speak about themselves in a negative way. By doing this, the listener believes that these things actually apply to you as well! Instead, try speaking calm and clear words saying exactly what you want them to know, not what they believe they already know.

Always show positivity for someone else, especially those who need it most, because Karma works very fast when we treat others kindly versus being mean or speaking negatively on purpose!

In every city or town there is a good and bad area. Learning how to identify which places will vibrate higher in frequency vs. the ones that drag your energy down is an important lesson for anyone who wants to attract positive things into their life!

If you're feeling like everything seems hard and difficult then it's time to see if you are living in a lower vibration home or neighbourhood, where negativity is running rampant much as germs from a sick person! If this sounds familiar look for somewhere new either online try to avoid going through real estate agents as they are usually motivated by only sales.

People with No Etiquette

If you are around people constantly who do not practice common courtesy then it's time to realize that you're probably being drained much in the same way mosquitoes suck the life from living creatures. This is because overly negative people will literally take energy away from those around them by how they communicate, oftentimes with bad language and other disrespectful ways.

Take into consideration how you feel when someone says something rude or nasty towards you; it's no wonder why someone might snap back and become defensive when this happens on a regular basis!

Your values are very important to how you feel about yourself and being able to recognize these low levels of frequency becomes easier as you learn more about yourself.

Keeping an open mind about life will help you better understand that we are all one and the same, with our own journey to travel upon this beautiful planet Earth.

It's not always easy to recognize low or high levels of vibrations but there are techniques that can help people flow with positive energy more often than before! The Law of attraction is a powerful tool because it helps you release negative things away from your life for good instead of continually going back time after time, basically creating a cycle of bad luck and failures. Remember that in order to find peace within yourself through making these changes you must first accept where you are now even if it's not quite where you want to be.

Watching or listening to things of a negative nature

Like television and magazines, can be a good indicator of where you are now in life. If there is too much negative media (and even music) around you then these low vibrational frequencies will simply be absorbed into your mind making things seem worse than they really are.

The best method or technique for learning how to vibrate higher is to change the way you think! Remember that we all have free will and everyone can make different choices each day, choosing love over hate instead of being judgmental towards someone else.

Understanding that karma plays an important role in how we feel every day it's very important.

Mistreating Yourself, Others, Animals, Or The Planet

Carelessness damages that energy vortex and brings negative things into the picture over time.

Try to practice consciousness regularly but use common sense when it comes to strenuous over-thinking activities; as such apply to go with the flow or vibe.

Mindless Activities

Limit your 'junk time' but don't be afraid to take a break either! Watching too much television can make things seem worse than they are. Try playing an instrument or using your creative superpowers instead of turning on the tube, turn off the computer and go for a walk in nature as often as possible.

Think of everything around you as energy that allows life this physical experience.

Drinking Alcohol

Alcohol can cause you to become even more stagnant or sedentary in your life and maintaining a dull hum of low vibrations. Avoid these types of situations as much as possible because they are not helpful to anyone, especially yourself!

While it may seem like fun go to parties every night it's actually very draining on the body physically and mentally when you realize that all of those late nights out keep you from being at the top of your game the next day.

A healthy dose is alright but too much partying is never good for the mind or body so be sure to give your liver a break once in a while, maybe put down the shots glass and find a healthier way to have fun instead!

Addictive behaviors

Simply put, distracting yourself with alcohol or drugs can be a good way to avoid your problems but do you really need to get so wasted every night just to feel better? It's very important that we all focus on understanding the power of our thoughts because this is where true change can begin in our lives when we realize that we can think positive and make different choices each day.

Eating Bad, Chemically Enhanced, Genetically Modified, And Highly Processed Foods And Animal Products

Food has an energy of its own and these types of foods are usually very bad for your health. Try to eat things that are as natural as possible because they're going to promote higher vibrations in the body, which allows you more energy, strength, and stamina.

Remember that every one thing you put into your body is sending a strong message around the universe about what types of things you want to attract back into your life so be sure to always make good choices when it comes to food!

Most people have no idea how important this is until something drastic happens like a serious illness or even worse death. Effortlessly following through with a healthy diet can help bring out the inner beauty and potential within ourselves without having to spend a ton on it.

Chapter 11:
How To Swiftly Shift Your Vibration

Raising your vibration and law of the attraction have become popularised in recent times. However, the essentiality, its processes and the need for it still remain a mystery to many.

The fact of the matter is that raising your vibration has more than one benefit attached to it and knowing exactly what benefits you could derive from raising your vibrational level can help in making better decisions on how to achieve this feat. Apart from all other advantages that you stand to gain by increasing your vibrational levels, here's a breakdown of some fast strategies on how you can shift your vibrations with ease:

Self-Acceptance

You might subscribe to yourself as 'unlucky' or someone who always seems to find more difficulties lying ahead in every step they take; but being self-aware of these hindrances contained within you makes you aware of them and therefore, gives you an opportunity to take measures to subvert them.

Self-acceptance can be attained by first overcoming your fears and insecurities that hinder the process of accepting yourself. Acknowledging these negative feelings attached with your life can help combat them over time; thereby reducing the number of times such a feeling surfaces within you while putting into practice self-love instead.

You see, successful vibrational shifts come from good personal relationships, which are initiated from love and care for yourself rather than love for others. This is why it's important to learn how to accept yourself before you embark on building positive relationships with people around you. A great place to start developing this skill would be through meditation and mindfulness training.

By bringing conscious awareness to your inner thoughts and feelings, you are able to recognize patterns of thought that may be preventing you from accepting yourself. Once these limiting thoughts have been identified, it is easier for you to work on changing them in the direction of inducing self-love rather than attracting negativity towards yourself. With time spent on meditative practices, it becomes easier for one to overcome fear through positive focus; thereby leading them toward attaining 'self-acceptance'.

Being More Optimistic

If there's anything in this world that can get anyone out of any mess at all, it's an optimistic attitude that keeps one going even when times get trying or worse still...downright frustrating! An optimistic mindset as opposed to being pessimistic.

Being optimistic attracts positivity into our lives; something that we have been striving to achieve through the practice of the law of attraction. Remember, your vibrational level is a reflection of how you feel about your life and everything in it and therefore...optimism allows us to attract more positive vibrations, which will ultimately lift up our vibrational levels.

Pessimists always expect the worst-case scenario to happen in any given situation while at the same time forgetting to consider any remedial measure that can counter such an outcome. It's important for us as human beings to stay on top by being prepared for what lies ahead even when there are factors (natural disasters, etc.) that may be out of our control yet be able to prepare well.

How To Tune Into Your Energy

To fully feel, know and understand your energy or vibration you are operating on you need to feel it for yourself. Therefore, to experience what energy you are flowing you can start by doing the below.

Step 1:

Find a comfortable seat or lying position and take a few minutes to focus on your breath. Once you mind has settled, start noticing how you feel; tense or relaxed? Racing thoughts or flowing ones?

Step 2:

Now tune into the most prominent emotion you feel right now. It doesn't matter if this is a positive or negative feeling, what matters is that you simply become aware of it. Noticing how the emotions feel in your body; heavy or light? Does it envelop your entire body (a whole) or does it just linger around one area? Try to describe this emotion with as much detail as possible by assigning color, texture size and weight to the feeling.

Step 3:

A journal is a great way to remember your private thoughts and feelings. The act of writing them down will help you engage with those emotions more deeply in the future, when it's time for personal growth.

Creating an inner language like this will be useful later on when you want to work with your energy more diligently.

<u>Now here's a good approach to changing or lifting your vibration after doing the above exercise;</u>

Step 1:

Close your eyes and remain still, take some deep breaths and allow yourself to relax for a few minutes (for beginners).

Step 2:

Once you are relaxed feel the space around you like you would were you to be sitting outside in nature.

Step 3:

Gently concentrate on what's surrounding you as if visualizing it; from how the air feels against your skin to how the earth smells after rain. The more time and attention spent on letting these thoughts flow within your being the easier it will be for you to 'feel' your energy.

A greater understanding of how vibrational levels affect us all is only possible through self-awareness of our own personal energies and vibrations; something that we must always keep in mind while practising this law.

Releasing Low Vibrational Energy

<u>Change Your Energy Field in Five Simple Steps:</u>

Step 1.

Be prepared to tune into the energy of your body, mind and spirit by desiring more attention in this regard.

Remember that tuning in means being able to feel out your spiritual energies; which will only happen if you put in regular practice towards making yourself more aware of such energies through meditation or activities that demand your focused attention on them (i.e. touch healing). The vibrations felt when meditating are feelings experienced as a result of connecting with the universal consciousness that's said to be made up of vibrating frequencies. So it follows...if you want to feel these 'frequencies', then it is best to understand how they are felt by first spending regular time learning how to meditate properly.

Step 2.

Be self-aware of the vibrations you feel throughout your body and know what they mean in relation to the true nature of your current state of being (mind, body and spirit).

Step 3.

Learn how to control these energies so that you can choose to align them with purposeful goals or positive feelings that will help work toward increasing their intensity as well as their vibrational level by using affirmations (I am...I have...I do...) and prayer.

Step 4.

Learn how to 'read' other people's energies too! This is a skill anyone can learn regardless of whether they are new to energy work or have been working on it for years.

Step 5.

Learn how to accept that all negative energies (and by extension, the 'people' whose vibrations they are) are a part of your knowledge and life path…just as positive ones will be too!

The more you align yourself with the energy vibration of self-love, the better able you become at seeing only the good in everything and everyone around you; thereby rendering any negativity useless because it no longer holds meaning for you in terms of its power to affect your emotions. Let me explain...when we choose to ignore what is negative about others (or even ourselves), when we simply detach ourselves from such thoughts and continue loving them instead...they have no power over us.

Manifesting Your Vibrational Frequency

When we want to increase our frequency, it is easy to see why most people reach for something that will change their vibration directly. Hypnosis (or guided visualizations) are a good tool for this because the words spoken and images shown during hypnotic states can be very powerful in helping you simply become more relaxed while you simply 'allow' positive change to flow into your being; especially when these same tools are used repeatedly...

This law is as old as time itself so there's no need for us to teach you how it works. The best we can do is provide some ideas that may prove useful if you're struggling with increasing your vibrational level at the moment...

<u>Here are seven practical ways, which have been proven effective in raising the vibration of your chakras and energy levels:</u>

1. Learn to meditate daily (or practice visualization techniques or creative visualization, which are close equivalents).

2. Connect with other people who have similar goals in life; share ideas and experiences with them in order to inspire each other or take up a challenge together against the negative influences that may be holding you back from experiencing higher vibrations all the time. You will find others like yourself once you open yourself to the universe and follow its energy.

3. Tap into Nature's positive energies by spending as much time as possible outdoors where nature lives in abundance

(this way, we can 'absorb' these natural frequencies through direct contact with the earth's natural energies).

4. Understand that while the vibrations you feel may be real and you may be able to 'feel' them, it doesn't mean your body has changed or that it is truly possible for anyone to experience higher frequencies even if they really wanted too! (This is also known as having a heightened sense of awareness or just being able to understand what others are thinking without them even saying a word.)

5. Direct all your thoughts toward positive solutions...energy follows thought so spend time thinking about the solutions which can help you transform negative energies into positive ones. For example: instead of trying to change someone who bothers or irritates you...find a way to tolerate him/her instead.

This is much easier than trying to change someone else...

6. Practice forgiveness and compassion toward everyone; especially those people who may seem as though they hate you: this way, you will be able to see how they are just the victim of some other person's negative energy (or even their own) and not really 'bad' at all. This way, you can begin to

accept them for who they are without thinking about changing them too!

7. Understand that a vague sensation of an unusual vibration isn't enough proof that something truly has changed within your chakras or your body either: just because you feel like things have changed doesn't mean that they actually have!

We can understand why some people would choose to believe just about anything that 'feels' true or makes them feel better instantly. Our minds are very 'suggestible' and we can often be convinced of achieving our goals if we simply try hard enough. The only problem with this kind of thinking is that it doesn't always last; because our focus isn't on things that truly matter like focusing on the constant improvement or constant growth of ourselves.

This book is not intended to harm anyone's beliefs...it's meant for people who are serious about understanding themselves more deeply so they can find a way to change their lives for the best by following an ancient law.

I know It's not easy to change...

Just imagine for one moment that you actually were able to vibrate higher at will and that it was possible for everyone to do so in reality too! It would mean that all of us can create 'anything' we want with just a single thought since we would be able to feel the right state of mind necessary to manifest this idea as a reality. We could literally change anything about ourselves or our bodies (like healing physical conditions like cancer, AIDS or heart disease), improve our relationships with others, increase our skills at work and earn more money too! There wouldn't be any need for politicians, laws, police officers or even lawyers because there simply wouldn't be any conflict within society anymore!

The only problem with this idea is that it's not possible for everyone to experience higher vibrations at will...we can't all be high vibrational! The reason why is because there are holes in our own energy field where we cannot receive or give either positive or negative energies. If we were able to feel a 'higher frequency' it would mean we eliminate these weaknesses and allow ourselves to experience life from both sides; rather than just the positive side of things like most people do today.

To transform our lives, we need to change....

It doesn't matter how much you believe in something (like being 'at one with nature or having a heightened sense of awareness) if you don't actually try and prove your beliefs first! I believe that everything in the universe has an equal and opposite reaction but this does not mean I will just believe it without trying to test this theory too!

There's a 'law of progress’, which is needed for our worlds (and ourselves) to grow and improve. If you want to experience success on your own terms then you need to understand why you are here...why you chose to incarnate at this time...what greater purpose exists within each one of us. In order for this plan to work, we all need to follow an ancient law that was 'lost' long ago in history: only a few chose to use or know about it while everyone else forgot how important it was. The problem with forgetting this particular law is that it can only be 'rediscovered' by ourselves...we need to remember it for our own reasons before we can discover what the original purpose was!

The law of progress states that there is no existing thing in this world that cannot be improved in some way. I believe that if you ever feel like things are meaningless or hopeless, then you are not following this law and a transformation from lower vibrations must take place within yourself first! If you want to experience more peace, happiness or anything else worth living for then you must find a way to change your life into something better than it was before. The only way I know how to do this is (without using drugs) is through reconnecting with nature or the universe itself; so we can reach a state of higher vibrations more often and more easily. The human body is energy activated...not just a physical shell full of water!

Because the universe is all about change, transformation and becoming something new (or better), it's vital that we don't get stuck in a rut where nothing seems to ever improve or evolve our lives too. If you find yourself wanting to 'check out' from society, then try reconnecting with nature so you can vibrate higher again! I noticed that when I'm around people or even watching certain types of movies on TV that my own vibration drops...the fast pace of life today makes me feel anxious sometimes since it's impossible for me to keep up with what everyone else wants from their lives.

How Raising Your Frequency Could Change Your World For The Better

We all vibrate at a particular frequency and so when we are in the same room together, our vibration picks up and connects to everyone else's frequency too. Because of this 'vibration attraction' which takes place on a subconscious level (through coherent resonance) an area can become unbalanced or polluted with lower vibrations! I have noticed that if I reconnect with old friends that I no longer want to speak with my own vibration becomes weaker...I feel more apathetic about life too. This is because I'm not 'seeing things from a higher perspective but instead absorbing all those bad feelings from other people who chose to put it out there for me to witness (instead of creating something better).

Because of this hidden effect, you might find yourself experiencing negative thoughts and emotions more often than before.

This is because essentially we either operate on positive or negative vibrations. These are the two opposite ends of one spectrum where zero is in the middle, some people consider 0 to be a 'void' while others think it's something more important than anything else. If we want to achieve balance (in life) then you must vibrate without any negative thoughts or emotions at all! If your vibration is low and you get caught up with other people's vices/negativity then you will often find yourself on a downward spiral because higher vibrations actually improve our lives in many ways!

Awakened people have been using this law for centuries...ever wondered why some people live such long, happy and healthy lives? I believe that they chose their right time to be of higher vibe and if they could live forever that would be ok.

Have you noticed how when you desire something with such intense energy the opposite is manifested? Well this is because you are in fact vibrating at a lower frequency and now the law brings you more of what you do not want. For example let's say someone is trying to break up with his or her partner but they can't stop 'thinking' about them...so they get even more attracted! But if that person somehow managed to release/let go of their relationship then they would eventually attract something better into their lives because in this world opposites are attracted...but it often takes an interval or time period before the higher vibrations take effect because the universe has many other plans for us too!

When we vibrate higher, things start to happen. Your energy will attract other people who have a similar vibration level too...we exist as energy not just physical flesh, there's no such thing as death (only transformation). Really think about this the next time you want something really badly because it can help you maintain your focus for a long enough amount of time so that your desire is manifested more easily.

Chapter 12: Raise Your Vibration For a More Fulfilling Life

We all have a set vibration frequency that we transmit and receive from others, this is why people who like each other 'attract' so easily. It's important to understand that you must always maintain a high vibration inside (no matter what life brings you) if you want to live a successful/fulfilling life! My advice for focusing on your own vibration level is to meditate daily...to lock into the right frequencies and achieve inner peace. Other spiritual ways to do this include dancing, chanting or just being with friends who are in tune with life too.

Some key principles in lifelong happiness are: - being good to people and animals - always thinking positively - choosing an optimistic attitude – even when it comes to bad news.

People who have mastered their emotions and accept themselves wholly are able to live freely, without suffering from unnecessary physical pain or emotional disturbance, stress or anxiety.

They have managed to achieve a state of inner strength and spiritual happiness that is not dependent upon the behaviour or attitude of others.

It's important to remember that we are all unique, each person vibrates at their own frequency but some people naturally run higher than others depending on certain life experiences. The result of this is some might seem 'on top' most of the time, while other people experience low vibrations more often than not. For example, if someone has experienced financial success at an early age and continue to live in luxury then they will likely hold on to such feelings for much longer because it becomes normal/habitual. In contrast; someone who rises from poverty to great wealth suddenly will probably feel like everything is impermanent...a result of their limited experiences.

All of this is to say that it's important to honor your emotions and not judge them, no matter how negative they feel; this will help you understand and respect yourself better. Your

intuition can be a very strong sense of guidance when you are in tune with your higher self/energy vibration. It's completely normal for people to have different perceptions depending on their frequency, as a result, they might make choices/judgements that may seem 'unfair' but never forget that we all have our own lessons to learn here on earth.
Even if an event seems horrible from the outside...there must be something good hidden somewhere in order for us to grow!

Before you can change, we should consider the previous steps:

A. Firstly, identify your vibrational level

B. Remove the frequency blockages

C. Start improving your vibration based on the ideas throughout this book.

Here are three short important steps for life-long vibe transformation:

1. get your mind right first, then you can design your life in a positive way

2. turn negative thoughts into positive ones

3. keep it up!

It's important to understand that you are not just stuck with the vibration level that you were born with, if you really want to change something about yourself...then it is possible with hard work and determination. No matter what challenges or obstacles come your way, don't let them block/slow down your journey for happiness at all costs!

Reasons To Raise Your Vibrational Frequency

There is a simple reason for why we vibrate high or low. It all comes down to how we feel about what happens in our life.

For example, your family just lost their jobs, so you are scared and worried that you will have no way of paying the bills...this translates into a lower vibration frequency (fear) which means that your energy levels will be on the negative side. If this feeling continues for long periods of time, it is almost impossible to change because it becomes normal behaviour! In contrast; If something good happens like getting an unexpected pay rise at work or winning some kind of lottery jackpot then your feelings are going to be elevated accordingly.

This is how we can lift our vibration to a higher level.

When you have managed to change your negative levels into positive ones then you will feel like the old self again, because everything has been reset! Just remember that it takes time for any new changes to take effect and persistent practice every day...but if you really want to make positive progress in life, these are the lessons that must be learnt!

There are lots of ways in which we can transform our negative energy into something more beautiful. For example; visualizations where we imagine light at the centre of our chakras (energy centers) filling up with golden bright lights or being surrounded by loved ones who love us unconditionally! These moments alone will help elevate our spiritvibration; there is no reason why you cannot feel like this all of the time.

Rather than getting angry with yourself, try to be positive about your current situation and learn from it! You don't necessarily need to have lots of money in order to live a great life because if you are happy within yourself then everything else will work itself out...the universe has plenty of amazing things for you if only you can believe enough! The secret is believing that they are possible in the first place which means releasing negative vibes, creating peace of mind and holding good thoughts always. This way we can start working our way up through the frequency levels until we reach something more beautiful/vibrant again.

Physical wellness

It is important for the vibrational frequency levels. For example; if you are ill or feeling weak from illness then this will inevitably lower your vibration level which means that you will feel limited in some way. It is time to look after ourselves by eating healthily, exercising and getting plenty of rest. Do not neglect your wellbeing because we always need to be in a good space mentally/physically! We become what we eat, so be careful how much junk food you eat as well as stay away from alcohol if it can harm your body/mind...remember that one day at a time works best with everything that is happening in life!

The human body is affected in so many ways. With increased blood flow, deeper breathing, stress alleviates and other bodily functions such as nervous system, digestion and sleep is affected positively. Physical activity helps to clear the mind and release any negative energies which might have built up over time.

Also, take some time for yourself to enjoy what life is really about!

Spiritual balance

When we are vibrating higher on a daily basis then it is much easier to live in the now moment-to-moment. The more relaxed you are, the less stressed out you will feel; this means that your overall vibration will increase naturally too! The idea of living happily in each day becomes easier because you have learnt from past experiences as well as putting effort into finding joy in everything again...this is why self-realization works best when we are feeling good about our lives first and foremost!

Attract more positive experiences

We can attract more positive experiences into our lives if we are vibrating higher overall. The goal is to never feel negative again because any negative emotions/thoughts will always bring us down. Therefore; the key is finding peace of mind in everything and being grateful for what you already have!

Learning How To Love Yourself First-And-Foremost

So many times people will neglect themselves for others...this isn't right as we all need time for self-reflection and regeneration! Remember that your greatest gift in life is YOURSELF so do not envy other people's success or happiness because YOUR time will come eventually.

Therefore, if you need to experience positive emotions alone then do it! And hopefully, on your journey, you will attract like-minded people along the way.

Align With Positive People

Try to surround yourself with good people by all means. This means that you have to be selective of who you choose as your friends because not everyone is ready for spiritual growth just yet so it can feel lonely in this process.

Therefore, the best way to align with positive beings is to hold high vibrational frequencies within yourself first-and-foremost; attract like-minded souls along the way and see where life takes you. It could even mean moving house or traveling somewhere new if necessary! But at least then, we will be surrounded by more well-balanced souls until we are able to raise our vibration levels ourselves. Good energy attracts good energy!

Access Greater Intuition

If we are in a relaxed state of being then intuition is heightened. The more that you 'zone-out' the easier it will be to tune into your feelings at all times; asking yourself yes or no questions helps also...such as when reflecting, 'Do I need more money?' See what answer comes to mind straight away!

Chapter 13: Spiritual Awareness

As we begin to wrap things up, I want to reiterate to you this book Vibrate Higher is a spiritual awareness book for those who are ready to explore their inner selves and work this practice regularly.

This inspirational read will help you remove negative energy to unlock your deepest, most beautiful self. Vibrate Higher can be used as a guide for finding peace within yourself by understanding that we are all one and the same with our own individual journeys on this planet.

Although the ultimate aim is to find peace we are conflicted because it's such a subjective term, especially when we are also to think about the human desires. It can be argued that living simply is the most peaceful option because we are in touch with our authentic selves; as humans, we have become used to a false persona, which has been created, from societal expectations and demands.

Why do we need to seek more material possessions?

Why do we crave recognition for our efforts?

These questions hold answers on how to vibrate higher!

It's not about suppressing desires or aiming for total elimination of negative feelings but rather at being able to cope and accept these emotions when they arise instead of becoming attached and overly involved. The first step is " acceptance" (I am where I am now) - feeling comfortable in whatever situation you find yourself.

Therefore, life becomes less stressful if you don't push yourself too hard to become perfect. Rather, letting go of judgmental thinking helps you feel more content with what is really important in your life; this will help you relax and Vibrate Higher.

One final question before we move onto the final conclusion, "Why not be happy with where you're at right now?" Wouldn't it be great if we could live in a society where people had real compassion for one another, instead of judging each other?

Maybe then people won't have to suffer or hurt themselves from negative emotions, which can occur when someone feels alienated because their desires aren't fulfilled. These ideals are held by our higher selves but let's keep them there for now -until we find balance within ourselves first.

We have become so dependent on the way that we think about things...to define what's right and wrong...maybe it is time to open up? We may not be able to change other people but if we can change our mindset then maybe then we can start to attract more like-minded people towards us. This is always a tricky situation because there are always going to be those who will judge you regardless of your intentions.

It's unhealthy when you are fearful of being judged as this disconnects from your soul's true nature and this can quickly attract negativity into your life.

Some people think that being spiritual means living an ascetic lifestyle; however, this is not true. You can still engage in activities from a perspective of enjoyment, you just need to ask yourself whether or not these actions are really fulfilling your inner desires.

A great way to find out is to take a break! Step back and assess if what you do gives you thrills beyond the momentary buzz? If it does then go for it; as long as it comes from purity and doesn’t harm anyone else,

Furthermore On Spiritvibration

In end, it's unhealthy when you are fearful of being judged as this disconnects from your soul's true nature and this can quickly attract negativity into your life. Your spiritvibration level is your best indicator of how you feel about yourself.

When you vibrate higher, you will find that people are attracted to you for the right reasons. A person who vibrates high will attract positive energy and will find it easier to forgive. When you vibrate higher, you will attract all things that can make you feel better. And when you feel better you attract things that enable you to vibrate higher.

It's a simple law and it works!

When we are happy with where we are right now, we stop becoming attached to achieving goals. Instead, we focus on what’s important to us, some people may phrase this as finding your passion, or calling in life, that's another conversation for another time. However, the main point is to focus on whats important to you regardless of the societal norms and this will enable you to find your purpose which helps to you vibrate higher daily.

This inner bliss is enhanced when you are surrounded by like-minded people, and this eventually brings out the hidden qualities within yourself. It's a blessing to be able to help others whilst enriching your own life, making it even more joyful for both parties involved.

When you connect with these positive feelings and emotions about what matters to you, you may feel confused but this is a natural process. Taking time to listen to your inner voice can be enlightening and if you listen when you are feeling confused, the answers will reveal themselves naturally.

When your vibration level increases, you also find that most of life's problems become small obstacles which makes it easier to open up and be around others. However, it's important to understand that you can still have times of sadness when some things don't go your way but this is not a cause for concern. Rather, if you are able to learn about yourself from these experiences then you will feel better in the long run.

When you energetically lift yourself up by vibrating higher, your surroundings will begin to change with more positivity and joy being felt by those around you. This is because we are all pure energy and therefore our frequency affects everything else around us. When you open yourself up to receiving more love from others then it's easier for you to vibrate higher.

There are many ways to start making things better for yourself and those around you, but to summarise: focus on what truly matters to you in life - your passions, enjoy time with family and friends (refrain from arguing), forgive others instead of holding grudges, try out new activities that interest you and stop worrying about what others will say or think.

When you do these things, with the right mindset, then your vibration level will start to rise and when you vibrate higher you begin to attract more positive energy and opportunities into your life! And through this it's important to remember one thing:

It's easier to vibrate higher when you feel loved and accepted by others. And it's also easier to love and accept those around you when you are happy with yourself, so start today!

Conclusion

Final words, we are not human beings having a spiritual experience, we are spirit beings having a human experience. Even though this is hard to understand for most people (myself included), it's important that you do try and remember this because your soul must be happy in order to vibrate higher on a daily basis.

You may find that there are some things in your life that do not feel right, but I promise you that with a little perseverance and time, everything will fall back into place. No matter what you choose to focus on in life, spend less time worrying about those things you have no control over and more time focusing on the love and peace which makes us happy.

If you try to find the happiness within yourself then you will begin vibrating higher on a daily basis and attract more positivity in your life.

And if you can do this, then we are all one step closer to living in a happier, spiritually connected world.

It's never too late to start vibrating at a higher level and the beauty of it is that you feel lighter within, so why not try it now?

And if you do feel like something is wrong, then it's probably because some aspect of your life needs improvement. Start with one thing and make it better today!

Vibrating at a higher level can help raise the vibration levels of those around you by using nature to your advantage. There are many ways to vibrate higher; such as meditating, exercising and eating healthy.

There are many spiritual teachers out there who help people to live a better life by vibrating higher. With their guidance, you can learn the ways of becoming more aware of your surroundings and the universe in order to have a happier life.

Vibrating at a higher level gives you insight into your life and helps you to understand the universe. By having this insight, you can learn how to become a better person in general. Knowing that there are many other ways of living your life, you can choose the best way for your specific needs by vibrating at a higher level.

As we all live out our lives every day, we must remember that we are all one and the same. We should not judge others, because no matter what, they are still living at their optimal vibration level for them.

When trying to learn how to vibrate higher every day, it is important to love yourself as much as you can. By doing this, everything will come together in your life.

In my final words on this, we began this book by talking about the interconnectedness of the mind, the thoughts that then are created into feelings and emotions, these vibrate at wavelengths that omit from each of us into the universe, and into all living things. The wavelength with which you operate and vibrate then attracts what it is your spiritvibration is unconsciously searching for. Therefore, be aware of what you think about and feel, as these emotions will create your reality. You can consciously choose the feelings that come into your life because of the thoughts you think.

So in order to vibrate higher daily practices must be applied to our lives. When we understand that the thoughts that come into your mind are from either yourself or another, do not fear these intruding thought-vibrations as they are only for a short while and will pass through you. It is how you respond to these vibrations that determines whether a good feeling or bad feeling develops in the body. We have mentioned many ways to deal with these thoughts and feelings in this book, find the one that works for you and your life.

For those of us who have either lost or never had a spiritual connection. There is nothing wrong with this because it does not mean you can't still be successful in life, nor that your life is lacking meaning or understanding. It only means that you need to learn how to do these things in order to discover your own spirituality. Each morning upon waking, before you get out of bed choose a thought, feeling and emotion that will be present throughout the day; like I am joyful, happy today! This way you set yourself up for success rather than failure by consciously projecting it into your day. Use this thought, feeling and emotion for the rest of your day.

Thoughts are not emotions, so don't let them become one. If a negative vibration intrudes on you, act positively until it leaves your mind, then find something at that moment to be happy about. This will change how you feel instantly and you can change how you feel by changing what you think about. If your body is in a bad state, let it go! Do not fear it, do not worry about the passing negative vibrations of others who are vibrating at lower levels than yourself. It will only hold you back and keep you from fully benefiting from your spiritual path.

If you can find a quiet spiritual place then go there often so that your energy levels are raised and you can think more clearly. Each one of us has our own way of learning, remembering and understanding.

Respect the vibrations that are found in nature, as these are the greatest spiritual levels you can achieve while on earth. Nature is abundant with life because all life is one and connected to itself! It is wise to spend time in nature, communing with it often to see the beauty that it holds and to understand how nature lives.

Many people in today's society have shut themselves off from this natural energy flow of life, trying to live their lives just as a machine works: mechanically. Deep down you don't want to be one of these people, and so find your vibration level as discussed in previous chapters, overcome those negative obstacles which you feel are holding you, as also described in this book and reconnect with your true vibrational level so you can be happier, attracting and doing what brings you joy, every day.

Keep in mind as you read this book and practice its principles that they work, so get going! Once you get started on your journey of vibrating higher daily, you will see results. The Universe is ready to give to those who believe in themselves and their dreams for the future because they are what the universe is made up of.

Thank You

Made in United States
North Haven, CT
12 June 2023

37618209R00090